Knitted Cats

Joy Gammon

SEARCH PRESS

Search Press Ltd
Wellwood, North Farm Road,
Tunbridge Wells, Kent TN2 3DR

An amalgamation of the following books first published by Search Press Limited, Tunbridge Wells:

Knitted Cats by Joy Gammon

Knitted Dogs by Joy Gammon

Photographs by Search Press Studios

The author would like to thank Anne Wilcox for all her help.

ISBN 0 85532 880 0

Printed and bound in Malaysia

The author

Joy Gammon studied biology and science at Studley College and Worcester College of Education, but her lifelong interest in knitting and design led her to the setting up of her own company and she is now a full-time knitwear designer, writer and broadcaster. She designs fashion and novelties for most UK and continental yarn manufacturers from initial concepts through to photography and printing. As well as being a regular contributor to a variety of craft and fashion magazines, Joy lectures for the Knitting Craft Group and to teachers. She is also a popular speaker a the Women's Institutes and various other women's groups.
She is the author of *All Stitched Up, Superknits, Dr Who Pattern Book, Play School Patterns* and *Large Print Knitting*, and is interested in all aspects of knitting and design.

This book is dedicated to all cat lovers everywhere.

Be they plain moggies or pampered thoroughbreds, all cats have great charm and character. I have tried to include a pet to suit all tastes and I hope you will enjoy making them as much as I did. Your finishing touches will give them their own highly individual personalities.

Joy Gammon

Introduction

Cats are strange, magical creatures and humans have always been fascinated by them. I like to think that, whereas dogs consider they are human, cats know that they are not but believe themselves to be our infinite superiors! We worship them, admire them and are allowed to look after them. Yet in spite of their aloofness, or perhaps because of it, and certainly because of their beauty and charm, we welcome them warmly as members of our family.

Many people collect cats, not just the real thing but china cats, stone cats, cloth cats, toy cats, painted cats, jewel cats and books on cats. To this you can now add knitted cats. From this book you can make your own versions of the ideal pet but you won't have to ask someone to feed them when you go away on holiday, nor deal with the well-intentioned dead mice offerings every morning. Whether your preference runs to a macho moggie, or a sophisticated Siamese, these fluffy knitted felines make wonderful toys, cushions and companions.

Tools and materials

Needles: exact knitting needle requirements are given in the instructions for each cat. Other requirements are stitch holders, row counters and blunt-ended sewing needles for seaming with wool (tapestry needles).

Yarns: see the individual patterns for exact requirements. The colours are your personal choice. You will need oddments of yarns for embroidering features and paws.

Filling: the cats are filled with washable man-made fibres. It is worth investing in this as home-made fillings, such as fabric oddments and cut-up stockings or tights, are often heavy and dark in colour and may show through the knitting.

Extras: safety eyes and noses for toys are available in various sizes and colours. All sorts of other extras may be added as the fancy takes you. The odd-eyed white kitten, for instance, has a pretty blue bow around her neck.

Stitches and abbreviations

Most of the cats are knitted in stocking stitch (abbreviated to st st), made by knitting and purling alternate rows, see page 30 for basic know-how. The other side is known as reverse stocking stitch (rev st st). Other general abbreviations used in this book are as follows:

alt	alternate(ly)
beg	begin(ning)
cont	continu(e)(ing)
dec	decreas(e)(ing)
DK	double knitting
foll	follow(ing)
gm	gram
inc	increas(e)(ing)
kg	kilogram
K	knit
K-wise	knit wise
M1	make one by picking up the loop which lies between the needles and knit through the back of the loop to increase a stitch
P	purl
rem	remain(ing)
rep	repeat
st	stitch(es)
tog	together
tbl	through back of loop

The numbers shown in parenthesis, ( ), refer to the larger size.

Sizes and tensions

All the cats featured in this book are made from three basic patterns: the lying down cat, the curled up cat and the sitting cat. Each pattern has two sizes and further size variations are achieved by using thicker or thinner yarns and their appropriate needles.

The patterns are set out in stitch and row numbers so that the proportions will remain correct however much the yarns vary. You, of course, can use the patterns with any yarn you wish at a suitable tension to achieve the size and colour of cat you desire. If you wish to use the yarns as given in this book, approximate tensions are shown in the individual cat patterns.

Knitting yarns quantities and conversions

Most yarns available in the UK are marketed by weight rather than by yardage. The density of dye used to obtain certain colours may result in more or less yarn in each ball, although the composition of yarn is exactly the same. The following conversions are provided as a guide:

$$25 \text{ gm} - 0.9 \text{ oz}$$
$$50 \text{ gm} - 1.8 \text{ oz}$$
$$100 \text{ gm} - 3.6 \text{ oz}$$

Methods and techniques

The three basic patterns: the main patterns and general finishing instructions for the lying down cat, curled up cat and sitting cat, are shown at the beginning of each section. Each basic pattern is followed by details of how the individual cat is created, giving the pattern and yarn details required to achieve the final effect. Instructions in the basic patterns are clearly listed in alphabetical sequence so that when you make your chosen pattern variation you can easily refer back to the basic instructions: as an example, the grey short-haired cat, shown on page 21, is in the lying down position and all the step-by-step instructions are listed under the basic pattern for this model, (see page 18). Only specific details of tools and materials stitch and feature variations, are given in the individual pattern (see page 20).

Making up and finishing: this is vitally important and can make all the difference between success and, at the best, peculiar results, so to help you with the finishing process each basic pattern has its own making up instructions. Always match shapings and ease any fullness in to match before seaming. I usually use back stitch for straight seams, and oversew the finished filled pieces together as invisibly as possible. Tease filling out well and do not over fill because knitting stretches and will distort, causing the filling to show.

Finishing touches

Remember to aim for caricature. Be as realistic as possible but with simplicity rather than fussiness. If possible, use a real cat as your model, or work from photographs or sketches. Believe what you see – cats' heads really are almost round and their surprisingly large ears do grow vertically from the sides of their heads.

Eyes: safety eyes are very realistic and successful and, of course, safe. Remember, though, to be quite sure of where you want to place them before attaching the washer at the back of the knitting, as they are virtually irremoveable. Most of the cats featured in this book have 'eye make-up' which creates an oval shape. Take a line of embroidery from the inner corner over to the outer corner of the eye. On many cats this line extends from the inner corner of the eye down to the outer edge of the nose and the nose itself is a darker colour (see Fig 1).

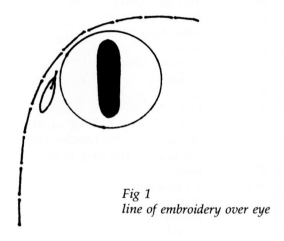

Fig 1
line of embroidery over eye

Noses: cats' noses are often pink, or of the same dark colour as their fur. I embroidered the characteristic petal-shape on to the cats' noses, (see Fig 2), and in some cases used a darker line of embroidery immediately below the main colour to enhance the nose shape. Safety noses are realistic and successful. I gave the grey short-haired cat a safety nose which shows up well on his dark colour.

Fig 2
embroidered nose

Muzzles: cats' muzzles divide immediately below the nose and, with straight stitches, this line can be added then divided into the characteristic inverted 'Y' shape which then curves up at either side, (see Fig 3), or remains straight and short on grumpy-faced breeds, (see Fig 4).

Fig 3
embroidered muzzle

Fig 4
embroidered muzzle for grumpy-faced breeds

Mouths: if you use a dark or black yarn for your cat, an added mouth may not be necessary as the seam is an effective mouth mark. But on lighter yarns an embroidered mouth adds character.

Whiskers: no cat is complete without its whiskers. These are usually white, and I have used ordinary yarn, cut into suitable lengths and stitched firmly on to the face at one end. I had to cut the lengths of yarn fairly short or the whiskers drooped, which is not suitable for all breeds of cat, although to some it adds character and a certain charm.

Ears: these are very important for both character and expression. Apart from the Persian and long-haired breeds whose ears tend to be an inverted 'V' the longest edge of most cats' ears is vertical to the side of the head. These then curve at the base to support the shape.

Watchpoint:
If the cats are to be given to small children, remember safety and ensure that all materials used are washable, non-toxic and that all trimmings are very firmly attached. Mohair and angora yarn are unsuitable for very small children.

Curled up cats

From the basic pattern for the curled up cat, make the tabby, the two playful kittens, the tortoiseshell and white cat and the white Persian.

Basic pattern

Body top and base (make two)

a) Cast on 20 (30) sts.

b) Inc one st at each end of every row until there are 32 (46) sts then inc one st at each end of every alt row until there are 40 (60) sts.

c) Work 14 (22) rows without shaping.

d) Dec one st at each end of next, then every alt row until 32 (46) sts remain.

e) Dec one st at each end of every row until 20 (30) sts remain.

f) Cast off.

Head

g) Cast on 8 sts and work 1 row.

h) Next row – Inc one st in every st (16) sts.
Work 1 row.

i) Next row – (Inc one st in next st, work 2, inc one st in next st) 4 times. (24) sts.
Work 1 row.
Next row – (Inc one st in next st, work 4, inc one st in next st) 4 times. (32) sts.
Work 1 row.

j) Cont in this way, adding 8 sts on every alt row by working 2 more sts between increasings on each increasing row, until there are 48 (72) sts.

k) Work 13 (19) rows without shaping.

l) Next row – *Work 2 tog, work 8 (14), work 2 tog tbl, rep from * to end. 40 (64) sts.

Work 1 row.
Next row – *Work 2 tog, work 6 (12), work 2 tog tbl, rep from * to end. 32 (56) sts.
Work 1 row.

m) Cont in this way, losing 8 sts on every alt row, and, so working 2 sts less between decreasings on each decreasing row until there are 8 sts.
Run a thread through rem sts.

Feet (make four)

n) Cast on 5 (7) sts and work 1 row.

o) Next row – Inc one st in every st. 10 (14) sts.
Rep the last 2 rows once more. 20 (28) sts.

p) Work 6 (8) rows without shaping.

q) *** Next row – *Work 2 tog, rep from * to end. 10 (14) sts.
Work 1 row.
Rep the last 2 rows once more.
Run a thread through rem 5 (7) sts.

Tail

r) Cast on 20 (28) sts.

s) Work 32 (48) rows without shaping.

t) Work as given for feet from *** to end.

Ears (make two)

Make one the reverse of the other.

u) Cast on 2 sts and work 1 row.

v) Inc one st at the same edge of every row until there are 8 sts.

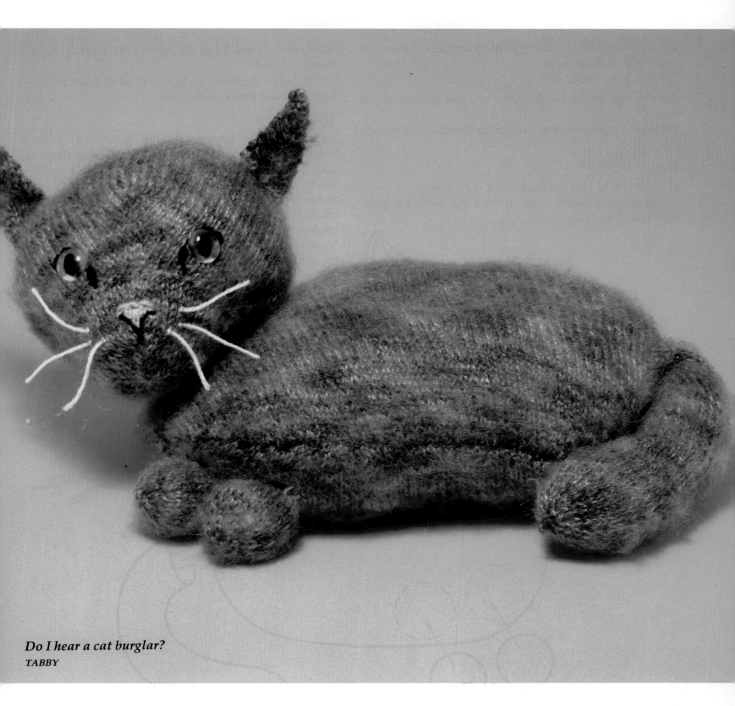

Do I hear a cat burglar?
TABBY

w) Dec one st at the same edge as before on every alt row until 2 sts remain.
Work 2 tog, fasten off.

Ear linings (make two): make one the reverse of the other.
Work as given for ears, but inc to 7 instead of 8 sts at v).

Nose

x) Cast on 32 (48) sts and work 6 (8) rows.
y) Next row – *work 2 tog, work 4 (8), work 2 tog tbl, rep from * to end.

Next row – *work 2 tog tbl, work 2 (6), work 2 tog, rep from * to end.
Continue to decrease in this way until 8 sts rem.
Run a thread through rem sts.

To make up

To assemble the pieces, (see Fig 5), work as follows:
Seam body top and base together matching shapings and fill before closing up. Seam head into a sphere, insert safety eyes, fill and attach to body.
Seam tail into a tube, fill and attach flat ended, also catching the tail down to the body of the cat if preferred. Seam feet into spheres and attach to body. Note that this cat can be positioned in various ways by adjusting the head and feet. The head can also be varied so that the cat is either looking up or at an angle. Stitch ear linings flat inside ears and attach ears to head.

Add details – see finishing instructions on page 6.

Fig 5

I feel like sleeping for 1001 nights
WHITE PERSIAN

Just taking a cat nap
TORTOISESHELL AND WHITE CAT

Tabby.

I gave this little tabby embroidered 'eye make-up' and strong white whiskers, (see page 9). She is approximately 38 cm (15 in) long.

Materials

Random-dyed DK, 3 × 50 gm balls in brown and black mix.
DK scraps for embroidery.
Approximately 250 gm (9 oz) washable filling.
1 pair medium sized safety cat's eyes.

Tension

22 sts and 28 rows = 10 cm (4 in) in st st on 4 mm needles. 4 mm needles are used throughout.

Pattern

Work as for basic pattern for curled up cat in st st throughout, making only 2 feet instead of 4.

Special notes: The pieces are brushed on the st st side before making up. I curled the cat's tail around her and attached it by the end, so that she only needs front feet as the back feet do not show.

Tortoiseshell and white

I used three colours to give a patchwork effect, (see opposite page). This cat is approximately 43 cm (17 in) long.

Materials

Mohair, 1 × 50 gm ball each of white, black and ginger.
DK scraps for embroidery.
Approximately 250 gm (9 oz) washable filling.
1 pair large sized safety cat's eyes.

Tension

18 sts and 24 rows = 10 cm (4 in) in st st on 4½ mm needles. 4½ mm needles are used throughout.

Pattern

Make the basic pattern for the curled up cat in the larger size in st st in the following colours:
Work the head in black.
Work 4 feet in any of the 3 colours.
Tail – cast on in black, work 15 rows in black at s), then 18 rows ginger, complete in white.
Ears – one white, one black.
Ear linings – one ginger, one white.
Nose – cast on and work 6 rows in ginger at x), complete in white.
Work the body top and base in large uneven areas patterned as you prefer in the three colours.

Special notes: Brush the st st side before making up and then assemble the cat in your chosen pose. I added strong white eyelines and whiskers, as well as multicoloured eyebrow whiskers, but she only needed a small dark nose.

White Persian

This cat is looking for a good home, (see page 11). Her approximate size is 43 cm (17 in) long.

Materials

Brushed chunky 2 × 100 gm balls in white.
DK scraps for embroidery.
Approximately 250 gm (9 oz) washable filling.
1 pair large sized safety cat's eyes.

Tension

14 sts and 18 rows = 10 cm (4 in) in st st on 6½ mm needles. 6½ mm needles are used throughout.

Pattern

Make the basic pattern for the curled up cat in the larger size in reversed st st, but making only 2 feet.

Special notes: Brush all the pieces on the reversed st st side before making up, and place the front feet under the chin so that the cat is curled round in a circle. Her face simply needs a pink nose and grey whiskers.

Playful kittens

These two little kittens are playful and mischievous, (see opposite page). Their approximate size is 30.5 cm (12 in) long.

Materials for black and white kitten

DK, 1 × 50 gm ball each in white and black.
Scraps of DK for embroidery.
Approximately 100 gm (4 oz) washable filling.
1 pair small sized safety cat's eyes.

Tension

24 sts and 32 rows = 10 cm (4 in) in st st on 4 mm needles. 4 mm needles are used throughout.

Pattern

Make the basic pattern for the curled up cat in the smaller size in st st throughout in the following colours:
Make the body top and base, the head and the ears in black. Make the feet, ear linings and nose in white. For the tail, cast on and work 24 rows in black, complete in white.

Materials for white kitten

Brushed DK, 1 × 50 gm ball in white.
Scraps of DK for embroidery.
Approximately 100 gm (4 oz) washable filling.
1 pair small safety cat's eyes.

Tension

As for black and white kitten.

Pattern

Make the basic pattern for the curled up cat in the smaller size in reversed st st throughout.

Special notes: These kittens are both illustrated in a sitting up position, ready to take on all-comers. You can also position them lying on their backs ready to play. The feet should then be stitched to the top of the body, the tail left straight, and the head facing upwards.

A purr-fect pair
TWO PLAYFUL KITTENS

Lying down cats

From the basic pattern for the lying down cat, make the grey short-haired cat, the odd-eyed white kitten, the long-haired kitten, the Siamese kitten and the rex.

Basic pattern

Body

a) Cast on 7 (10) sts and work 1 row.

b) Next row – Inc one st in every st, 14 (20) sts.
Work 1 row.

c) Rep the last 2 rows twice more. 56 (80) sts.

d) Work 40 (66) rows without shaping.

e) Next row – *Work 2 tog, rep from * to end.
Work 1 row.

f) Rep the last 2 rows twice more.
Run a thread through rem 7 (10) sts.

Head

g) Cast on 8 sts and work 1 row.

h) Next row – Inc one st in every st. (16) sts.
Work 1 row.

i) Next row – (Inc one st in next st, work 2, inc one st in next st) 4 times. (24) sts.
Work 1 row.
Next row – (Inc one st in next st, work 4, inc one st in next st) 4 times. (32) sts.
Work 1 row.

j) Cont in this way, adding 8 sts on every alt row by working 2 more sts between increasings on each increasing row, until there are 48 (72) sts.

k) Work 13 (19) rows without shaping.

l) Next row – *Work 2 tog, work 8 (14), work 2 tog tbl, rep from * to end. 40 (64) sts.
Work 1 row.
Next row – *Work 2 tog, work 6 (12), work 2 tog tbl, rep from * to end. 32 (56) sts.
Work 1 row.

m) Cont in this way, losing 8 sts on every alt row, and so working 2 sts less between decreasings on each decreasing row until there are 8 sts.
Run a thread through rem sts.

Legs and feet (make four)

n) Cast on 20 (28) sts.

o) Work 26 (40) rows without shaping.

p) Next row – *Work 2 tog, rep from * to end.
Work 1 row. 10 (14) sts.

q) Rep the last 2 rows once more.
Run a thread through rem 5 (7) sts.

Tail

r) Work as given for legs and feet, but work 32 (48) rows straight at o).

Ears (make two)

Make one ear the reverse of the other.

s) Cast on 2 sts and work 1 row.

t) Inc one st at the same edge of every row until there are 8 sts.

u) Dec one st at the same edge as before on every alt row until 2 sts remain.
Work 2 tog, fasten off.

Ear linings (make two): one the reverse of the other. Work as given for ears, but inc to 7 instead of 8 sts at t).

Nose

v) Cast on 32 (48) sts and work 6 (8) rows.
w) Next row – *Work 2 tog, work 4 (8), work 2 tog tbl, rep from * to end.
Next row – *Work 2 tog tbl, work 2 (6), work 2 tog, rep from * to end.
Continue to decrease in this way until 8 sts rem.
Run a thread through rem sts.

To make up

To assemble the pieces, (see Fig 6), work as follows:
Seam body piece into a tube and fill before closing up, placing this and all other seams downwards. Seam legs and tail into a tube, leaving cast on edge open. Fill and attach legs flat ended beneath body. Fill and attach tail open ended.
Seam head into a sphere, insert safety eyes, fill and attach to the body. Note that the position of the head can be varied to that the cat is looking up, forward or at an angle. Seam side edges of nose, fill and attach to head by the cast on edge.
Stitch ear linings flat inside ears and attach ears to head.
Add detail – see finishing instructions on page 6.

Fig 6

19

The grey short-hair.

This cat is lanky but otherwise very plain and his approximate size is 38 cm (15 in) long (see opposite).

Materials

Brushed DK, 2 × 50 gm balls in dark grey.
DK scraps for embroidery.
About 150 gm (5 oz) of washable filling.
1 pair medium safety cats' eyes and 1 medium safety nose.

Tension

24 sts and 32 rows = 10 cm (4 in) in st st on 4 mm needles. 4 mm needles are used throughout.

Pattern

Make the basic pattern for the lying down cat in the smaller size, but add 12 extra rows to the body at d), the legs at o), and the tail at r), working in st st throughout.

Special notes: I gave this cat a safety nose which shows up well on his dark colour, and then stitched white whiskers in to his ears for added character.

Long haired kitten

This little kitten needs to be brushed every day, (see opposite). She is approximately 30.5 cm (12 in) long.

Materials

Brushed DK, 2 × 40 gm balls in grey.
DK scraps for embroidery.
Approximately 100 gm (4 oz) washable filling.
1 pair medium safety cat's eyes.

Tension

22 sts and 28 rows = 10 cm (4 in) in st st on 4 mm needles. 4mm needles are used throughout.

Pattern

Make the smaller size of the basic pattern for the lying down cat, in reversed st st throughout.

Special notes: The reversed st st pieces are brushed, and I added fairly strong features that show up on the grey, including a dark area above the nose, and pale 'eyebrows'.

Siamese kitten

This kitten's 'eye make-up' gives her the oriental look, (see opposite). Her size is approximately 28 cm (11 in) long.

Materials

DK, 1 × 50 gm ball in beige, and a small quantity of chocolate brown.
DK scraps for embroidery.
Approximately 100 gm (4 oz) washable filling.
1 pair small blue safety cat's eyes.

Tension

24 sts and 32 rows = 10 cm (4 in) in st st on 4 mm needles. 4 mm needles are used throughout.

Pattern

Make the basic pattern for the lying down cat in the smaller size in st st in the following colours:
Body, head and ear linings in beige, nose and ears in brown.
Legs and feet – cast on and work the first 20 rows at o) in beige, complete in brown.
Tail – cast on and work the first 20 rows in beige in the same way, complete in brown.

Special notes: Make up matching the colours and then add strong dark lines around the eyes and nose to give the distinctive oriental look.

A basketful of mischief
LONG HAIRED GREY KITTEN
GREY SHORT HAIRED CAT
AND SIAMESE KITTEN

Smile please
REX AND THE ODD–EYED KITTEN

Odd-eyed white

This pretty little odd-eyed kitten has a blue satin bow around his neck, (see opposite). He is approximately 43 cm (17 in) long.

Materials

Brushed DK, 1 × 100 gm ball in white.
DK scraps for embroidery.
Approximately 250 gm (9 oz) washable filling.
1 pair medium safety cats eyes *in odd colours*.
Length of satin ribbon.

Tension

24 sts and 32 rows = 10 cm (4 in) in st st on 4mm needles. 4 mm needles are used throughout.

Pattern

Make the larger size of the basic pattern for the lying down cat, in st st throughout.

Special notes: The pieces for this kitten were firmly brushed before making up, and he has distinctive odd eyes. I found he needed very little embroidery, just a pink nose, brown mouth and eye markings and white whiskers.

Rex

The rex was knitted in 'crunchy' yarn, (see opposite), and his approximate size is 35.5 cm (14 in) long.

Materials

DK slub, 3 × 50 gm balls in cream.
DK scraps for embroidery.
Approx 150 gm (5 oz) washable filling.
1 pair medium safety cat's eyes.

Tension

24 sts and 32 rows = 10 cm (4 in) in st st on 4 mm needles. 4 mm needles are used throughout.

Pattern

Work as for basic pattern for lying down cat in the smaller size, in reversed st st.

Special notes: Reversed st st in the crunchy yarn gives a very authentic rex feel. I added only simple, darker embroidery lines at the sides of the nose.

Sitting cats

From the basic pattern for the sitting cat, make the Siamese, the Persian, the ginger tom and the black and white cat.

Basic pattern

Front of body

a) Cast on 36 (54) sts and work 24 (36) rows without shaping.**

b) Next row – Work 2 tog, work to end.
Next row – Work to last 2, work 2 tog.
Next row – Work 2 tog, work to end.
Next row – Work without shaping.

c) ***Rep the last 4 rows until 18 (28) sts rem.
Work 1 row.
Cast off.

Back of body

d) Work as given for front of body as far as **.

e) Next row – Work to last 2, work 2 tog.
Next row – Work 2 tog, work to end.
Next row – Work to last 2, work 2 tog.
Next row – Work without shaping.

f) Complete as given for front of body from *** to end.

Head

g) Cast on 8 sts and work 1 row.

h) Next row – Inc one st in every st. (16) sts.
Work 1 row.

i) Next row – (Inc one st in next st, work 2, inc one st in next st) 4 times. (24) sts.

Work 1 row.

Next row – (Inc one st in next st, work 4, inc one st in next st) 4 times. (32) sts.

Work 1 row.

j) Cont in this way, adding 8 sts on every alt row, by working 2 more sts between increasings on each increasing row, until there are 48 (72) sts.

k) Work 13 (19) rows without shaping.

l) Next row – *Work 2 tog, work 8 (14), work 2 tog tbl, rep from * to end. 40 (64) sts.

Work 1 row.

Next row – *Work 2 tog, work 6 (12), work 2 tog tbl, rep from * to end. 32 (56) sts.

Work 1 row.

m) Cont in this way, losing 8 sts on every alt row, and so working 2 sts less between decreasings on each decreasing row until there are 8 sts.

Run a thread through rem sts.

Feet (make four)

n) Cast on 5 (7) sts and work 1 row.

o) Next row – Inc one st in every st. 10 (14) sts.

Rep the last 2 rows once more. 20 (28) sts.

p) Work 6 (8) rows without shaping.

q) ***Next row – *Work 2 tog, rep from * to end. 10 (14) sts.

Cats' chorus
BLACK AND WHITE CAT, SIAMESE AND GINGER TOM

Fig 7

Work 1 row.
Rep the last 2 rows once more.
Run a thread through rem 5 (7) sts.

Tail

r) Cast on 20 (28) sts.
s) Work 32 (48) rows without shaping.
t) Work as given for feet from *** to end.

Base

u) Cast on 13 (20) sts.
v) Inc one st at each end of every row until there are
33 (48) sts.
Work 1 row.
w) Dec one st at each end of every row until 13 (20) '
sts remain.
Cast off.

Ears (make two)

Make one the reverse of the other.

x) Cast on 2 sts and work 1 row.

y) Inc one st at the same edge of every row until there are 8 sts.

z) Dec one st at the same edge as before on every alt row until 2 sts remain.

Work 2 tog, fasten off.

Ear linings (make two): make one the reverse of the other.

Work as for ears, but inc to 7 instead of 8 sts at y).

Nose

aa) Cast on 32 (48) sts and work 6 (8) rows.

bb) Next row – *work 2 tog, work 4 (8), work 2 tog tbl, rep from * to end.

Next row – *work 2 tog tbl, work 2 (6), work 2 tog, rep from * to end.

Continue to decrease in this way until 8 sts rem.

Run a thread through rem sts.

To make up

To assemble the pieces, (see Fig 7), work as follows:

Seam body halves together, matching shaping, insert base and fill before closing up.

Seam head into a sphere, insert safety eyes, fill and attach, noting that the angle of the head can be varied as you wish.

Seam feet into spheres, fill and attach to body. Seam tail into a tube, fill and attach to body open ended.

Stitch ear linings flat inside ears and attach ears to head.

Add details – see finishing instructions on page 6.

Blue Persian

This kitten needs to be brushed vigorously to give the Persian look, (see page 25). He is approximately 25.5 cm (10 in) high.

Materials

Brushed chunky, 2 × 100 gm balls in grey.

DK scraps for embroidery.

Approximately 400 gm (14 oz) washable filling.

1 pair large safety cat's eyes.

Tension

14 sts and 18 rows = 10 cm (4 in) in st st on 6½ mm needles. 6½ mm needles are used throughout.

Pattern

Make the smaller size from the basic pattern for the sitting cat in st st with the following variations:

Work 30 rows without shaping on the body pieces at a).

Work 23 rows without shaping on the head at k).

Work 6 rows without shaping on the nose at aa).

Special note: I added frown lines between the eyes and an unsmiling mouth to give the Persian expression. The nose is pink, and there are matching white whiskers in the ears.

Black and white

This cuddly cat needs very little detail added, (see page 29). His approximate size is 28 cm (11 in) high.

Materials

Brushed DK, 1 × 100 gm balls each of black and white.

DK scraps for embroidery.

Approximately 200 gm (7 oz) washable filling.

1 pair medium safety cat's eyes.

Tension

24 sts and 32 rows = 10 cm (4 in) in st st on 4 mm needles. 4 mm needles are used throughout.

Pattern

Make the smaller size from the basic pattern for the sitting cat in st st in the following colours:
Work ear linings, nose and feet in white.
Work base and ears in black.
Cast on and work the first 16 rows of the tail in black, complete in white.
Front of body – work the first row at a): 26 sts black, 10 sts white. Keep these sts in these colours throughout the rem of the work, so working a white strip up the unshaped edge.
Back of body, as for front of body, *but* work the first row 10 sts white, 26 sts black, so making this piece the reverse of the front.

Special note: brush all the pieces and match colours where applicable. This cat's markings make him so striking that he needed no more detail than a pink nose and white whiskers.

Ginger tom

This cat has tiger-like markings and long whiskers, (see opposite). He is approximately 23 cm (9 in) high.

Materials

Random-dyed DK, 1 × 50 gm ball in ginger-orange mix.
DK scraps for embroidery.
Approximately 200 gm (7 oz) washable filling.
1 pair medium sized safety cat's eyes.

Tension

22 sts and 28 rows = 10 cm (4 in) in st st on 4 mm needles. 4 mm needles are used throughout.

Pattern

Make the smaller size from the basic pattern for the sitting cat in st st.

Special note: To give the tigerish expression I added strong stripes outside the eyes, white lines below the eyes and brown eyebrows. The mouth and nose are a strong, dark brown, and the whiskers are long.

Siamese

The Siamese's eyes are embroidered in blue and she is wearing a new red collar, (see opposite). She is approximately 33 cm (13 in) high.

Materials

DK, 1 × 50 gm ball in beige, plus a small quantity of chocolate brown.
DK scraps for embroidery.
Approximately 200 gm (7 oz) washable filling.
Collar.

Tension

24 sts and 32 rows = 10 cm (4 in) in st st on 4 mm needles. 4 mm needles are used throughout.

Pattern

Make the larger size of the basic pattern for the sitting cat in the following colours and variations:
Work the body in beige, casting on only 46 sts for the front and back at a), and decreasing down to 20 sts at c).
Work the head and ear linings in beige.
Work the nose, ears and feet in brown.
Work the first 40 rows of the tail at s) in beige, complete in brown.

Special notes: I embroidered the distinctive oriental eyes in blue rather than using the toy safety eyes, and I added eyelines in brown and a strong nose marking in beige. The nose is pale, and the whiskers are as long as possible.

Dalmatian puppy

The characteristic spots are simply chain stitched on to give this dog his distinctive dalmatian character, (see opposite). He is approximately 28 cm (11 in) high.

Materials
Crepe DK, 2 × 50 gm balls in white.

DK scraps for embroidery in black.
Approximately 200 gm (7 oz) washable filling.
1 pair medium sized safety dog's eyes and 1 medium safety dog's nose.

Tension
24 sts and 32 rows = 10 cm (4 in) in st st on 4 mm needles. 4 mm needles are used throughout.

Pattern
Make the smaller size of the basic pattern for the seated dog with no variations.

Special notes: This dog is, of course, spotted. I worked the spots in black in chain st though some dalmatians have liver brown spots. These marks vary in size and are evenly spread all over his body. His ears are attached with a fold at the back.

Pattern
Make the smaller size of the basic pattern for the seated dog, in cream throughout and in st st.

Special notes: the ears have a small fold at the back to give shape. I added typical labrador 'eyebrows'.

Tailpiece

Making these dogs gave me a great deal of pleasure. I do hope you enjoy just as much as I did creating any of these variations and varieties. Be they mutts or mastiffs, Heinzes or Harlequins, pups or Pulis, – I'm sure that someone will love them dearly.

Helping hand

If you are a complete beginner at knitting, or your skills are a little rusty, the following information will be helpful.

Place the needle holding the stitches in the left hand and hold the working needle and the yarn in the right hand. Control the yarn by winding it round the fingers of the right hand, (see Fig 8).

Fig 8 controlling the yarn tension

Casting on

Begin with a slip loop about 15 cm (6 in) from the end of the yarn and tighten it on to the left-hand needle (see Fig 9). Insert the right-hand needle into the front of the loop, left to right, wind the yarn round the right-hand needle point and draw it through to the front (see Figs 10 and 11). Transfer the loop from the right-hand needle to the left-hand needle. Continue in this way, but insert the needle *between* the stitches on the left-hand needle, (see Fig 12), until you have the correct number of stitches.

To knit stitches

Hold the yarn at the back of the work. Insert the right-hand needle into the first stitch on the left-hand needle from front to back, left to right (see Fig 13). This is known as 'knitwise'. Pass the yarn round the right-hand needle point, (see Fig 14) and draw the loop through to the front of the work, (see Fig 15). Slip the stitch off the left-hand needle (see Fig 16). Continue in this way along the row until you have transferred all the stitches to the right-hand needle. Turn the work and hold it in the left hand in preparation for the next row.

To purl stitches

With the yarn at the front of the work, insert the right-hand needle into the front of the first stitch on the left-hand needle from right to left (see Fig 17). This is known as 'purlwise'. Pass the yarn round the right-hand needle point (see Fig 18). Draw the loop through (see Fig 19), then slip the stitch off the left-hand needle (see Fig 20). Continue in this way along the row.

Fig 9 casting on   *Fig 10*   *Fig 11*   *Fig 12*

Knit stitch

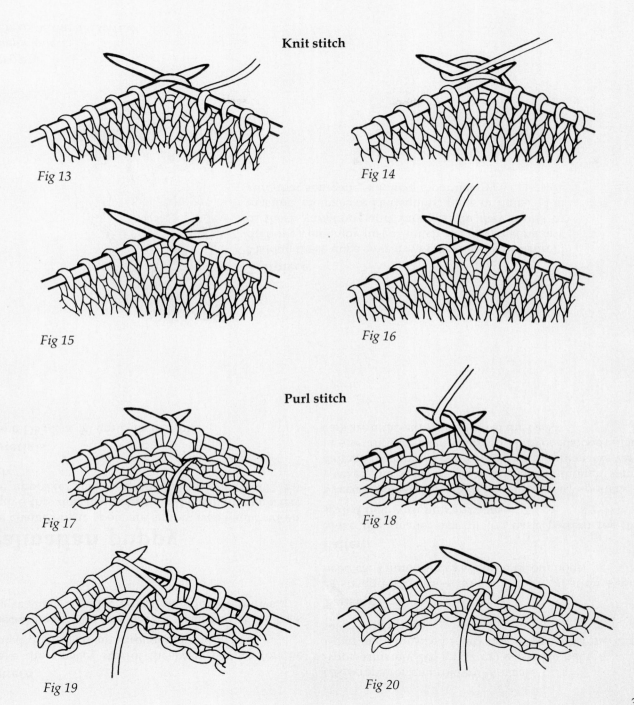

Fig 13

Fig 14

Fig 15

Fig 16

Purl stitch

Fig 17

Fig 18

Fig 19

Fig 20

31

Feline blue
PERSIAN

Knitted Dogs

Joy Gammon

SEARCH PRESS

Introduction

Ever since my childhood dogs have been part of our family. Whether a much-loved mongrel from a dog's home or an equally loved Crufts winner, they have all had a special relationship with us, and knitting their cuddly portraits seemed an obvious thing for me to do.

Knitted dogs have tremendous charm. The choice of breed, size and colour is all yours without difficult decisions such as, 'Is an Afghan quite the thing in our high rise flat?' or 'Can I bear to spend hours grooming an Old English sheepdog every day?' These dogs really do *sit*! They do not moult (well , not much anyway), and they do not eat a great deal, so go ahead and knit as many as you like. If you get overrun they make marvellous presents.

Tools and materials

Needles: exact knitting needle requirements are given in the instructions for each dog. Other requirements are stitch holders, row counters and blunt-ended sewing needles for seaming with wool (tapestry needles).

Yarns: see the individual patterns for exact requirements. The colours are your personal choice. You will need oddments of yarns for embroidering features and paws.

Filling: the dogs are filled with washable man-made fibres. It is worth investing in this as home-made fillings, such as fabric oddments and cut- up stockings or tights, are often heavy and dark in colour and may show through the knitting.

Extras: safety eyes and noses for toys are available in various sizes and colours. All sorts of other extras may be added as the fancy takes you. The miniature poodle, for instance, is wearing a blue 'diamond-studded' collar and a matching ribbon in her hair. A small amount of pink felt, or ribbon, for your dog's tongue, adds instant appeal.

Stitches and abbreviations

Most of the dogs are knitted in stocking stitch (abbreviated to st st), made by knitting and purling alternate rows. The other side is known as reverse stocking stitch (rev st st). Other general abbreviations used in this book are as follows:

alt	alternate(ly)
beg	begin(ning)
cont	continu(e)(ing)
dec	decreas(e)(ing)
DK	double knitting
foll	follow(ing)
gm	gram
inc	increas(e)(ing)
Kg	kilogram
K	knit
K-wise	knitwise
M1	make one by picking up the loop which lies between the needles and knit through the back of the loop to increase a stitch
P	purl
rem	remain(ing)
rep	repeat
tog	together
tbl	through back of loop

The numbers shown in parenthesis, ( ), refer to the larger size.

Sizes and tensions

All the dogs featured in this book are made from three basic patterns: the lying down dog, the sitting dog and the standing dog. Each pattern has two sizes except for the standing dog, which does not work in a larger size. Further size variations are achieved by using thicker or thinner yarns and their appropriate needles.

The patterns are set out in stitch and row numbers so that the proportions will remain correct however much the yarns vary. You, of course, can use the patterns with any yarn you wish at a suitable tension,

to achieve the size and colour of dog you desire. If you wish to use the yarns as given in this book, approximate tensions are shown in the individual dog patterns.

Methods and techniques

The three basic patterns: these main patterns and the general finishing instructions for the lying down dog, the sitting dog and the standing dog, are shown at the beginning of each section. Each basic pattern is followed by details of how the individual dog is created, giving the pattern and yarn details required to achieve the final effect. Instructions in the basic patterns are clearly listed in alphabetical sequence so that when you make your chosen pattern variation you can easily refer back to the basic instructions: as an example, the Afghan hound puppy, shown on page 16, is in the lying down position and all the step-by-step instructions are listed under the basic pattern for this model, (see page 14). Only specific details of tools and materials, stitch and feature variations are given in the individual pattern (see page 19).

Making up and finishing: this is vitally important and can make all the difference between success and, at the best, peculiar results, so to help you with the finishing process each basic pattern has its own making up instructions. Always match shapings and ease any fullness in to match before seaming. I usually use back stitch for straight seams, and oversew the finished stuffed pieces together as

invisibly as possible. Tease filling out well and do not over fill because knitting stretches and will distort causing the filling to show.

Finishing touches

As always with knitted toys and portraits, remember to aim for caricature. Be as realistic as possible, but with simplicity rather than fussiness. If possible, work from the real thing, or photographs and drawings, and believe what you see. Poodles really do have ears attached half way down the sides of their heads and dalmatians do have random spots of different sizes. Safety eyes and noses are very successful, realistic and safe. Remember though to be quite sure of where you want to place them before attaching the washer on the back, as they are virtually irremoveable.

Mouths: if you use a dark or black yarn for your dog, a knitted mouth may not be necessary as the seam is an effective mouth mark. But on lighter yarns an embroidered mouth adds character. Dogs' muzzles divide immediately below the nose and, with straight stitches, this line can be added then divided into the characteristic 'Y' shape. Left straight this gives the typical effect of the more aggressive and terrier breeds, (see Fig 1).

A slight curve and extended backwards line gives an impression of charm and friendliness, (see Fig 2), but avoid a teddy bear smirk as this is not a typical doggy expression, (see Fig 3).

Fig 1
embroidered muzzle for assertive breeds   *embroidered muzzle for friendly breeds*

Fig 2

Fig 3
incorrect embroidered muzzle

Felt or ribbon tongues of the correct pink can be added, but need to be attached so that they flop in true canine fashion.

Noses: safety noses are very realistic and successful and, of course, safe. Remember, though, to be quite sure of where you want them before attaching the washer on to the back of the knitting, as they are virtually irremovable.

Eyes: the realistic safety eyes must be placed carefully and accurately. Most of the dogs featured in this book have 'eye make-up' which creates an oval or round shape. Take a line of embroidery from the inner corner over to the outer corner of the eye for the oval-eyed breeds, (see Fig 4a). For round-eyed breeds add a dark 'V' of embroidery at either side of the eye (see Fig 4b), and experiment with lighter colours on the darker coloured or black dogs. A curve of white immediately below the eye gives a soulful look while some breeds and individuals have eyebrows, either marked as tufts or splashes of colour, which can be copied.

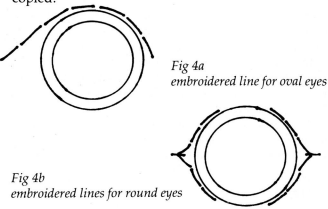

Fig 4a
embroidered line for oval eyes

Fig 4b
embroidered lines for round eyes

Ears: these are important and indicate both character and expression. Ears which flop or turn over always have a fold towards the back, at the attached edge, so that they stand away from the head. Pricked ears are made by curving the base to support the shape and the outer edge is usually vertical.

Claws: if required, these are simply four contrasting straight stitches on each paw.

Markings: spots and head markings can be embroidered afterwards with chain stitch or Swiss darning and can be placed in whatever position suits you and your dog.

Watchpoint:
If the dogs are to be given to small children, remember safety and ensure that all materials used are washable, non-toxic and that all trimmings are very firmly attached. Mohair and angora yarn are unsuitable for very small children.

Knitting yarn quantities and conversions

Most yarns available in the UK are marketed by weight rather than by yardage. The density of dye used to obtain certain colours may result in more or less yarn in each ball, although the composition of yarn is exactly the same. The following conversions are provided as a guide:

25 gm	– 0.9 oz
50 gm	– 1.8 oz
100 gm	– 3.6 oz

to achieve the size and colour of dog you desire. If you wish to use the yarns as given in this book, approximate tensions are shown in the individual dog patterns.

Methods and techniques

The three basic patterns: these main patterns and the general finishing instructions for the lying down dog, the sitting dog and the standing dog, are shown at the beginning of each section. Each basic pattern is followed by details of how the individual dog is created, giving the pattern and yarn details required to achieve the final effect. Instructions in the basic patterns are clearly listed in alphabetical sequence so that when you make your chosen pattern variation you can easily refer back to the basic instructions: as an example, the Afghan hound puppy, shown on page 16, is in the lying down position and all the step-by-step instructions are listed under the basic pattern for this model, (see page 14). Only specific details of tools and materials, stitch and feature variations are given in the individual pattern (see page 19).

Making up and finishing: this is vitally important and can make all the difference between success and, at the best, peculiar results, so to help you with the finishing process each basic pattern has its own making up instructions. Always match shapings and ease any fullness in to match before seaming. I usually use back stitch for straight seams, and oversew the finished stuffed pieces together as

invisibly as possible. Tease filling out well and do not over fill because knitting stretches and will distort causing the filling to show.

Finishing touches

As always with knitted toys and portraits, remember to aim for caricature. Be as realistic as possible, but with simplicity rather than fussiness. If possible, work from the real thing, or photographs and drawings, and believe what you see. Poodles really do have ears attached half way down the sides of their heads and dalmatians do have random spots of different sizes. Safety eyes and noses are very successful, realistic and safe. Remember though to be quite sure of where you want to place them before attaching the washer on the back, as they are virtually irremoveable.

Mouths: if you use a dark or black yarn for your dog, a knitted mouth may not be necessary as the seam is an effective mouth mark. But on lighter yarns an embroidered mouth adds character. Dogs' muzzles divide immediately below the nose and, with straight stitches, this line can be added then divided into the characteristic 'Y' shape. Left straight this gives the typical effect of the more aggressive and terrier breeds, (see Fig 1).

A slight curve and extended backwards line gives an impression of charm and friendliness, (see Fig 2), but avoid a teddy bear smirk as this is not a typical doggy expression, (see Fig 3).

Fig 1
embroidered muzzle for assertive breeds

Fig 2
embroidered muzzle for friendly breeds

Fig 3
incorrect embroidered muzzle

Felt or ribbon tongues of the correct pink can be added, but need to be attached so that they flop in true canine fashion.

Noses: safety noses are very realistic and successful and, of course, safe. Remember, though, to be quite sure of where you want them before attaching the washer on to the back of the knitting, as they are virtually irremovable.

Eyes: the realistic safety eyes must be placed carefully and accurately. Most of the dogs featured in this book have 'eye make-up' which creates an oval or round shape. Take a line of embroidery from the inner corner over to the outer corner of the eye for the oval-eyed breeds, (see Fig 4a). For round-eyed breeds add a dark 'V' of embroidery at either side of the eye (see Fig 4b), and experiment with lighter colours on the darker coloured or black dogs. A curve of white immediately below the eye gives a soulful look while some breeds and individuals have eyebrows, either marked as tufts or splashes of colour, which can be copied.

Fig 4a
embroidered line for oval eyes

Fig 4b
embroidered lines for round eyes

Ears: these are important and indicate both character and expression. Ears which flop or turn over always have a fold towards the back, at the attached edge, so that they stand away from the head. Pricked ears are made by curving the base to support the shape and the outer edge is usually vertical.

Claws: if required, these are simply four contrasting straight stitches on each paw.

Markings: spots and head markings can be embroidered afterwards with chain stitch or Swiss darning and can be placed in whatever position suits you and your dog.

Watchpoint:
If the dogs are to be given to small children, remember safety and ensure that all materials used are washable, non-toxic and that all trimmings are very firmly attached. Mohair and angora yarn are unsuitable for very small children.

Knitting yarn quantities and conversions

Most yarns available in the UK are marketed by weight rather than by yardage. The density of dye used to obtain certain colours may result in more or less yarn in each ball, although the composition of yarn is exactly the same. The following conversions are provided as a guide:

25 gm – 0.9 oz
50 gm – 1.8 oz
100 gm – 3.6 oz

Standing dogs

The basic pattern for the standing dogs, with variations, makes the West Highland White terrier, the Jack Russells, the cross-breed terrier and the long haired terrier.

Basic pattern

Main body piece

This is worked in one piece from tail end towards head, with two legs on each side. The work is folded down the middle at the back to make the dog shape.

a) Cast on 78 sts. Work in st st, inc one st at each end of every alt row until there are 86 sts.
Work 2 rows without shaping.

b) Dec one st at each end of every alt row until 78 sts rem. Work 1 row without shaping.

c) Shape back legs. Cast off 10 sts at beg of next 2 rows.

d) Shape body. Work without shaping on rem 58 sts for 40 rows.

e) Shape one front leg and half the head. Cast on 10 sts at beg of next row and work 39 sts, (including the 10 sts cast on).
Put rem sts on a holder.
Turn and complete this side first.

f) Cast on 16 sts at beg of next row, noting that these cast on sts form the beg of the head.
Inc one st at each end of every alt row 4 times.

g) Work 3 rows without shaping.

h) Keeping head edge straight, dec one st on every alt row at the foot edge 4 times, finishing at the foot edge.

i) Shape front leg. Cast off 29 sts at beg of next row, work to end.

j) Shape face. Dec one st at each end of every row 6 times.

k) Cast off 6 sts at beg of next row.
Work 2 rows without shaping.

l) Dec one st at beg of next and every foll alt row until 9 sts rem, then cast off.

m) Pick up sts from holder and work to match, reversing all shapings to complete the other side of the dog.

Main underbody gusset

n) Cast on 3 sts, and work 1 row.
Note: This cast on edge is the front of the gusset.

o) Work in st st inc one st at each end of every alt row until there are 13 sts.

p) Work 20 rows without shaping.

q) Shape inside leg – **Cast on 10 sts at beg of next 2 rows.

r) Inc one st at each end of every alt row 4 times. Work 2 rows without shaping, (41 sts).

s) Dec one st at each end of every alt row 4 times.

t) Cast off 10 sts at beg of next 2 rows.**

u) Inc one st at each end of every alt row until there are 17 sts.
Work without shaping for 36 rows.

v) Dec one st at each end of every alt row until 13 sts rem.
Work 1 row.

w) Rep from ** to **. (13 sts).

Fig 5

x) Work without shaping for 10 rows.
y) Dec one st at each end of next, then every alt row until 3 sts rem.
Work 3 tog, cast off.

Head gusset

z) Cast on 3 sts and inc one at each end of every 4th row until there are 15 sts.
Work without shaping for 10 rows.
aa) Dec one st at each end of every alt row until 3 sts rem.
Work 3 tog, cast off.

Ears (make 2)

bb) Cast on 16 sts and work 12 rows without shaping.
cc) Shape tip of ears. Dec one st at each end of every row until 4 sts rem. Cast off.

Tail

dd) Cast on 16 sts and work 12 rows without shaping.
ee) Dec one st at each end of every row until 2 sts rem.
Work 2 tog, fasten off.

To make up

To assemble the pieces, (see Fig 5), work as follows:
Double main body piece, join top of nose and insert head gusset between back of nose and head division with the wide part, (cast off end), to the front. Insert base gusset, matching legs and easing ends in so that cast on edge joins front of nose and cast off end joins centre of back. Insert safety eyes and nose and fill. Double tail, fill and attach. Attach ears.
Add detail – see finishing instructions on page 3.

Life's a ball!
WEST HIGHLAND WHITE TERRIER

Jack Russell terriers

These two little terriers are happy and playful, although they can be mischievous too (see opposite). Their approximate size is 35.5 cm (14 in) long.

Materials for white Jack Russell

DK, 1 × 50 gm ball in white.
Scraps of brown and black DK.
Approximately 150 gm (5 oz) washable filling.
1 pair medium sized safety dog's eyes and 1 medium safety dog's nose.
Silver yarn.
Silver button.

Tension

24 sts and 32 rows = 10 cm (4in) in st st on 4 mm needles. 4 mm needles are used throughout.

Pattern

Make basic pattern for standing dog in white and st st throughout.
Work 1 ear in brown, altering ears by working 6 rows without shaping at bb), instead of 12.
Cast on the tail in brown and work the first 8 rows in brown, then complete in white.

Materials for brown Jack Russell

DK, 1 × 50 gm ball in brown.
Small quantity of white DK.
Scrap of black DK.
Approximately 150 gm (5 oz) washable filling.
1 pair medium sized safety dog's eyes and 1 medium safety dog's nose.
Silver yarn.
Silver button.

Tension

As given for white Jack Russell

Pattern

Make basic pattern for standing dog in st st in colours as follows:
Main body piece brown.

Main underbody gusset in white.
Head gusset in white.
One ear in black, one ear in white, altering row number at bb), to 6 instead of 12.
Tail – Cast on in black, work 6 rows in black, 2 rows in brown and complete in white.

Special notes: these are happy little dogs so I added curved mouth shapes and expressive eyebrows. The white dog has a large black dot embroidered on his back, and each dog has a crocheted 'chain' in silver yarn and a silver button as a tag. Ears are folded, and tails are vertical, terrier style.

West Highland White terrier

Despite his tough appearance, this dog has a soft heart. I have added a smart traditional tartan collar to make him feel at home, (see page 9). He is approximately 35.5 cm (14 in) long.

Materials

Brushed angora look DK, 2 × 40 gm balls in white.
DK scraps for embroidery.
Approximately 250 gm (9 oz) washable filling.
1 pair medium sized safety dog's eyes and 1 medium safety dog's nose.
Tartan collar.

Tension

22 sts and 28 rows = 10 cm (4 in) in st st on 4 mm needles. 4 mm needles are used throughout.

Pattern

Work as for basic pattern for standing dog in reversed st st.

At bb), on the ears, work only 4 rows without shaping, instead of 12.

Special notes: the pieces are brushed on the reversed st st side before making up. Westies have vertical tails and their ears are curved at the bottom, but without a fold, to give a pointed upright effect. They have fluffy eyebrows, with whiskers beneath the eye as well, and they have a tough expression, so do not curve the mouth too high.

Cross breed terrier

This scruffy, loveable dog makes a comforting companion, (see opposite). His approximate size is 35.5 cm (14 in) long.

Materials

Random-dyed DK, 2 × 50 gm balls in brown.
DK scraps for embroidery.
Approximately 250 gm (9 oz) washable filling.
1 pair medium sized safety dog's eyes and 1 medium safety dog's nose.

Tension

22 sts and 28 rows = 10 cm (4 in) in st st on 4 mm needles. 4 mm needles are used throughout.

Pattern

Make the basic pattern for the standing dog in reversed st st.

At bb), on the ears, work only 8 rows without shaping, instead of 12.

Special notes: brush the reversed st st side before making up to give the authentic 'scruffy' look. The ears are folded at the base, but droop, and the eyes have a soulful white line.

Long haired terrier

This terrier can look scruffy unless he is groomed regularly (see page 6). He is approximately 43 cm (17 in) long.

Materials

Mohair, 3 × 50 gm balls in brown.
DK scraps for embroidery.
Approximately 250 gm (9 oz) washable filling.
1 pair medium sized safety dog's eyes and 1 medium safety dog's nose.

Tension

16 sts and 22 rows = 10 cm (4 in) in st st on 5½ mm needles. 5½ mm needles are used throughout.

Pattern

Make the basic pattern for the standing dog in reversed st st.

Special notes: because it is mohair, this yarn can be really well brushed before making up, and 'groomed' afterwards. Attach ears with a pleat, and the tail flat and pointing downwards.

Let me tell you a shaggy dog story
AFGHAN HOUND PUPPY

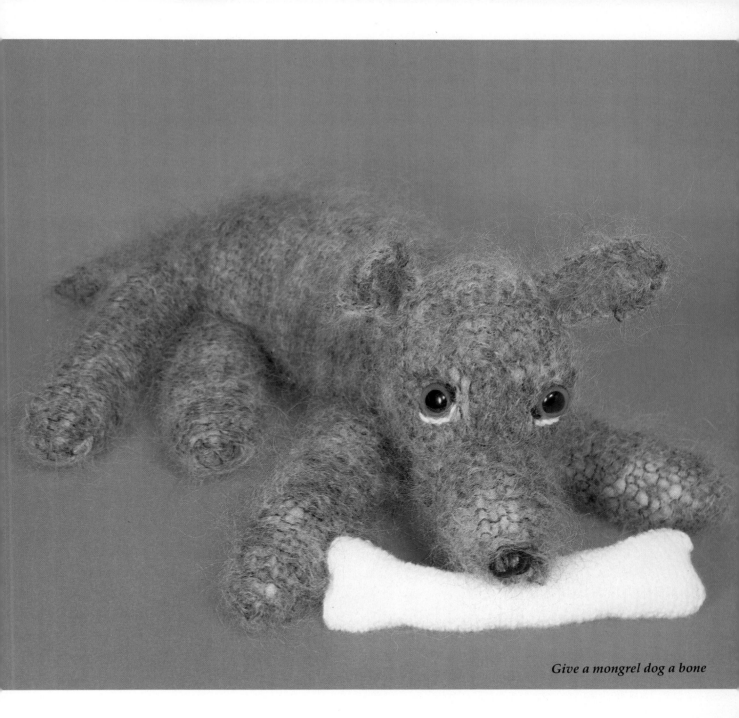

Give a mongrel dog a bone

Afghan hound puppy

Our Afghan hound puppy is approximately 76 cm (30 in) long, and has been made in a cut fur stitch (see previous page). The loops are cut when work is complete, to give a realistic fur effect. However, the puppy will 'moult' if not handled gently, so if you intend to make this model for a younger child, do not cut the loops as instructed.

Materials

Brushed chunky, 5 × 100 gm balls in pale brown. DK, 1 × 50 gm ball in brown.
DK scraps for embroidery.
About 1 kg (2lb) of washable filling.
1 pair large safety dog's eyes and 1 large safety dog's nose.

Tension

15 sts and 22 rows = 10 cm (4 in) in st st on 5½ mm needles. 5½ mm needles are used throughout.

Pattern

Make the basic pattern for the lying down dog in the larger size but working the nose in DK yarn used double in st st and working the last 8 rows of the legs also in st st in DK yarn used double, i.e. at g) work only 21 (33) rows in fluffy chunky, cont to end in st st in double DK.
Work all of the remainder in fluffy chunky in cut fur st as follows:
Row 1 – (Right side) K.
Row 2 – K1, *insert tip of right hand needle K-wise into next st, wind yarn twice around 3 fingers of left hand, K the st from the left hand needle, K the yarn from around the fingers without removing the fingers, pass the first of these 2 sts over the 2nd, K the next st, remove fingers, rep from * to last 2 sts, K2.
Row 3 – K.
Row 4 – K2 rep from * as given for row 2 to last st, K1.
Work all pieces in this st pattern, keeping it correct throughout all shaping and noting that fur st can variably affect the tension, so ensure that the body piece is roughly square before casting off.

When work is complete, insert scissors into the loops, pull and cut loops centrally, to give fur effect.

Special notes: fur stitch is very stretchy so take care not to overfill. Sewing up fur st is difficult because all the loops get in the way, but the finished effect is well worth it. The ears are attached almost flat at the head sides.

Rough coated mongrel

This dog looked in need of love and affection, so I knitted him a nice, juicy bone (see opposite). He is approximately 51 cm (20 in) long.

Materials

Mohair, 2 × 50 gm balls in brown.
DK scraps for embroidery.
Approximately 250 gm (9oz) washable filling.
1 pair medium sized safety dog's eyes and medium safety dog's nose.

Tension

15 sts and 19 rows = 10 cm (4 in) in st st on 6½ mm needles. 6½ mm needles are used throughout.

Pattern

Make the smaller size of the basic pattern for the lying down dog, in reversed st st throughout.
At v), on the ears, work only 6 (10) rows without shaping.

Special notes: because he is a mongrel, this dog is slightly assymetric with ears attached in different ways, each folded at the base, and he has a soulful look, with white under the eyes. His bone is a rectangle, seamed into a bone shape and filled.

Toy poodle

I added charm to this little poodle by tying a blue bow around her neck (see opposite). She is approximately 33 cm (13 in) long.

Materials

Brushed DK, 1 × 50 gm ball in peach.
DK scraps for embroidery.
Approximately 250 gm (9oz) washable filling.
1 pair medium safety dog's eyes and 1 medium toy safety dog's nose.
Length of ribbon.

Tension

24 sts and 32 rows = 10 cm (4 in) in st st on 4 mm needles. 4 mm needles are used throughout.

Pattern

Make the larger size of the basic pattern for the lying down dog in reversed st st throughout except for the nose which should be made in st st, and the last 8 rows of the legs which should also be in st st, i.e. work 21 (33) rows in reversed st st. Change to st st to complete.
Head – Work as given as far as o).
Before p), work as follows:
Next row – Work 1 *M1, work 2, rep from * to end. 61 (85) sts.
Work 17 rows without shaping at p).
Next row – Work 1 *work 1, work 2 tog, rep from * to end.
Work as given from q).
At k), work only 8 (10) rows without shaping for the tail.
Pom-pon for tail – Cast on 5 sts.
P 1 row.
Next row – In K, inc one st in every st (10) sts.
Rep the last 2 rows (20) sts.
Work 9 rows without shaping.
Next row – K2 tog to end.
P 1 row.
Next row – K2 tog to end.

Run a thread through rem sts and use to seam into a ball, then fill and attach to end of tail.

Special notes: the reversed st st areas are brushed, to give a slightly furry look, and a blue satin ribbon is stitched on around the neck.

Chihuahua

The chihuahua is very simple and quick to make, and he is the smallest of all the dogs featured in this book, (see opposite). He is approximately 17.5 cm (7 in) long.

Materials

DK crepe, 1 × 50 gm ball in white.
DK scraps for embroidery.
Approximately 100 gm (4 oz) washable filling.
1 pair small safety dog's eyes and 1 small safety dog's nose.

Tension

24 sts and 32 rows = 10 cm (4 in) in st st on 4 mm needles. 4 mm needles are used throughout.

Pattern

Make the basic pattern for the lying down dog in the smaller size in st st.
Work only 4 (6) rows at v), for the ears.
Head – Work as given as far as o), then work as follows:
Next row – Work 1, *M1, work 2, rep from * to end.
Work 13 rows without shaping at p).
Next row – Work 1, *work 1, work 2 tog, rep from * to end.
Work as given from q).

Special notes: the ears are placed upright with curved bases and no turn over or fold.

OPPOSITE:
Let sleeping dogs lie
TOY POODLE AND CHIHUAHUA

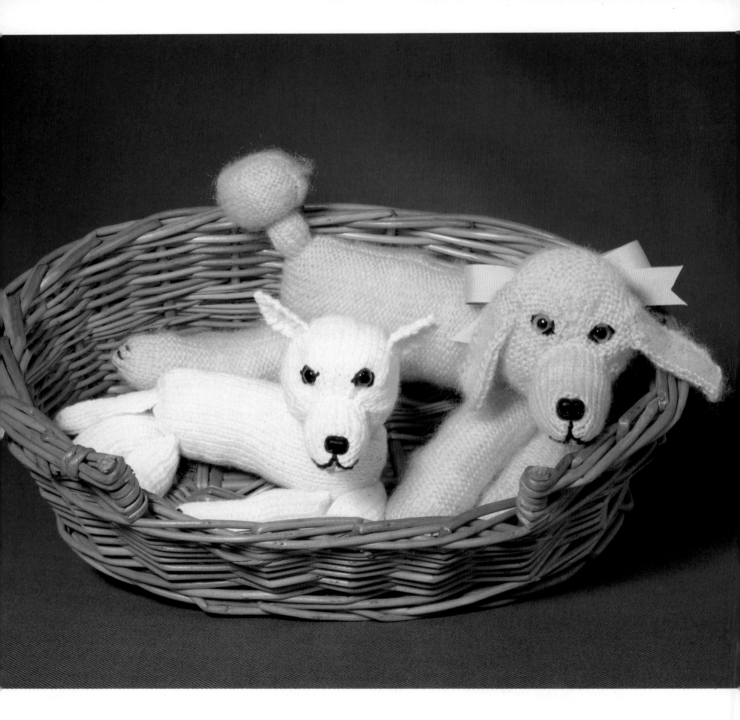

Sitting dogs

The basic pattern for the seated dogs, with variations, makes the labrador, the poodle, the Old English sheepdog, the dalmatian and the border collie.

Basic pattern

Main body piece

a) Cast on 72 (108) sts.
b) Work 36 (54) rows without shaping.
c) Dec one st at each end of the next, then every foll alt row until 52 (78) sts rem.
d) Dec one st at each end of every foll row until 22 (32) sts rem.
e) Work 1 row and cast off.

Base gusset

f) Cast on 18 (26) sts.
g) Inc one st at each end of every row until there are 24 (36) sts, then every alt row until there are 30 (46) sts.
h) Work 1 row.
i) Dec one st at each end of next, then every alt row until there are 24 (36) sts, then every row until 18 (26) sts rem.
Cast off.

Tail

j) Cast on 20 (32) sts.
k) Work 36 (54) rows without shaping.
l) **Next row – *Work 2 tog, rep from * to end. 10 (16) sts.
Work 1 row.
Rep the last 2 rows once more. 5 (8) sts.
Run a thread through rem sts.**

Back paws (make two)

m) Cast on 20 (32) sts.
n) Work 8 (12) rows without shaping.
o) Work as given for tail from ** to **.

Front paws (make two)

p) Cast on 5 (8) sts.
Work 1 row.
Next row – Inc one st in every st to end. 10 (16) sts.
Work 1 row.
Next row – Inc one st in every st to end. 20 (32) sts.
q) 10 (14) rows without shaping.
r) Work as given for tail from ** to **.

Nose

s) Cast on 30 (46) sts.
t) Work 8 (12) rows without shaping.
u) Dec one st at each end of the next, then every foll row until 16 (26) sts rem.
Cast off.

Ears (make two)

v) Cast on 10 (14) sts.
w) Work 8 (12) rows without shaping.
x) Dec one st at each end of next, then every alt row until 4 (6) sts rem.
Cast off.

To make up

To assemble the pieces, (see Fig 7), work as follows:

Double the main piece and seam, matching shapings and colours if applicable, leaving the base, (cast on edge), open for filling. Insert safety eyes. Insert gusset and fill.

Seam back paws and tail into a tube, leaving the cast on edge open. Fill and attach with straight ends of paws flat under the body, and with tail open ended. Seam front paws into a sphere, fill and attach. Double nose and seam matching shapings, leaving cast on edge unseamed, insert safety nose, fill and attach. Attach ears. Add detail – See finishing instructions on page 3.

Fig 7

then 16 white rows, then completing the work in black.

Nose, from the cast on edge onwards, throughout the work, work the centre 6 sts in white, the rem in black.

Gusset in black.

Special notes: match the characteristic markings when making up, and add an irregular embroidered white stripe between the eyes. I highlighted the inner eye corners with white, and added a pink floppy tongue.

Border collie

The border collie loves doggy yarns and long walks and is looking for a caring owner (see front cover). He is approximately 30.5 cm (12 in) high.

Materials

Brushed DK, 1 × 100 gm ball in white and 1 × 100 gm ball in black.

DK scraps for embroidery.

Approximately 300 gm (11 oz) washable filling.

1 pair large sized safety dog's eyes and 1 large safety dog's nose.

Scrap of pink felt.

Tension

24 sts and 32 rows = 10 cm (4 in) in st st on 4 mm needles. 4 mm needles are used throughout.

Pattern

Make the smaller size of the basic pattern for the seated dog with the following variations:

All four paws in white.

Ears in black.

Tail, cast on and work first 24 (30) rows in black, then complete in white.

Main body piece, cast on in black and work straight rows at b), in black.

Commence shaping, working 8 further black rows

Old English sheepdog

This dog can be brushed to give a fluffy look, although I have given him a smooth coat, (see opposite). He is approximately 46 cm (18 in) high.

Materials

Brushed chunky, 2 × 100 gm balls in white and 1 × 100 gm ball in grey.

DK scraps for embroidery.

Scrap of pink felt.

Approximately 500 gm (1 lb 2 oz) washable filling.

1 pair large sized safety dog's eyes and 1 large safety dog's nose.

Tension

14 sts and 18 rows = 10 cm (4 in) in st st on 6½ mm needles. 6½ mm needles are used throughout.

Pattern

Make smaller size from the basic pattern for the seated dog with the following variations:-

No tail.

Make all four paws, the nose and ears in white.

On the main piece, from the beg onwards, work the centre 16 (24) sts in white, with 28 (42) sts in grey at either side.

When the 36 straight rows at b) are complete, work the shaping as given, *at the same time*, inc the number

Feeling dog-eared
MINIATURE POODLE

of white sts in the centre by one each side on every row until no more sts in grey rem.
Cont and complete in white.
Work gusset in grey.

Special notes: the ears are almost flat on the side of his head and I have added a pink felt floppy tongue.

Miniature poodle

This black poodle has a 'diamond-studded' collar and matching bow, (see opposite). She is approximately 40.5 cm (16 in) high.

Materials
Brushed DK, 3 × 50 gm balls in black.
Approximately 300 gm ((11 oz) washable filling.
1 pair large sized safety dog's eyes and 1 large safety dog's nose.
Dog collar.
Length of ribbon.

Tension
24 sts and 32 rows = 10 cm (4 in) in st st on 4 mm needles. 4 mm needles are used throughout.

Pattern
Work as for the basic pattern for the seated dog, in the larger size with the following variations:
Work main body piece and ears in reversed st st and work 12 (18) rows without shaping at w), instead of 8 (12) rows for the ears.
Work nose and paws in st st.
Work tail in st st working only 8 (12) rows without shaping at k), then cast off.
Work one extra 'front paw' in reversed st st to act as bobble on the end of the tail.

Top knot
Cut a strip of very thin card about 20.5 cm (8 in) long by 10 cm (4 in) wide, depending on the size of top knot you wish your poodle to have. Leaving a short length of yarn free, wind the yarn loosely along the length of card for the required thickness, then leaving an end of about 30.5 cm (12 in) cut the yarn and thread it into a blunt-ended wool needle. Insert the needle through the loops at one card-edge, going under 3 or 4 loops at the same time and bringing the needle up and back over these loops to form a firm back stitch. Continue along the card-length until all the loops are secured (work another row of back stitch if required).

Remove the card from the loops by bending slightly then insert the needle through all the loops at once, but do not pull up too tightly. Now bring one end of the secured loops round in a circle to meet the other end and fasten off securely by tying the first short end of yarn and use the remainder of the yarn to sew the pom-pon on to the poodle's head. Tie a ribbon around the top knot in a pretty bow, and stitch on.

Special notes: brush reversed st st areas, and make up the bobble into a sphere to add to the end of the tail. This dog is such a dense black I added no embroidery, as this would not have shown, but treated her to a smart new collar instead.

Labrador puppy

This loveable little pup is looking for a good home (see page 28). Her approximate size is 25.5 cm (10 in) high.

Materials
DK, 2 × 50 gm balls in cream.
DK scraps for embroidery.
Approximately 200 gm (7 oz) washable filling.
1 pair medium sized safety dog's eyes and 1 medium safety dog's nose.

Tension
24 sts and 32 rows = 10 cm (4 in) in st st on 4 mm needles. 4 mm needles are used throughout.